INVESTING FOR KIDS

Building a Strong Financial Future
for Your Kids

Walter D. Hood

Table of contents

INTRODUCTION

Introduction to Investing for Kids

Investing is a way of making your money grow by putting it into stocks, bonds, mutual funds, or other financial instruments. Investing can be a great way for kids to learn about the world of finance and how to manage their money.

Here are some key concepts to introduce kids to when it comes to investing:

Compound interest: This is the idea that the money you invest will earn interest, which in turn will earn more interest over time. Compound interest can make your money grow much faster than simple interest.

Diversification: This means spreading your investments across different types of assets, such as stocks, bonds, and mutual funds. Diversification can help reduce risk by avoiding putting all your money in one investment.

Risk and return: All investments come with some level of risk, but the higher the risk, the higher the potential return. It's important to understand the balance between risk and return when making investment decisions.

Long-term thinking: Investing is a long-term strategy, so it's important to have patience and avoid making impulsive decisions based on short-term fluctuations in the market.

Start early: The earlier you start investing, the more time your money has to grow. Even small amounts of money invested over a long period of time can make a big difference.

Introducing kids to investing can be a great way to teach them important financial concepts and help them build a strong financial foundation for their future. It's important to start with small amounts of money and seek advice from a trusted financial advisor when making investment decisions.

Why it's important to teach kids about investing

Teaching kids about investing is important for several reasons:

Financial literacy: By teaching kids about investing, we can help them develop financial literacy skills that they can use throughout their lives. This includes learning about concepts like compound interest, risk management, and diversification.

Long-term financial planning: Investing is a key component of long-term financial planning. By teaching kids about investing early on, we can help them understand the importance of setting financial goals and creating a plan to achieve them.

Wealth creation: Investing is one of the most effective ways to create wealth over time. By teaching kids about investing, we can help them understand the power of investing and how it can help them achieve their financial goals.

Life skills: Investing requires a range of skills, including critical thinking, analysis, and decision-making. By teaching kids about investing, we can help them develop these skills, which will be useful in all areas of their lives.

Financial independence: Investing can be a key tool for achieving financial independence. By teaching kids about investing, we can help them understand how to build and grow their wealth over time, which can lead to greater financial independence and security in the future.

Teaching kids about investing is an important part of their financial education and can help set them up for a successful financial future.

Basic concepts and terms

Here are some basic concepts and terms in investing that kids can learn:

Investing: Investing means putting your money into something with the expectation of earning a profit. In the context of personal finance, investing often refers to buying stocks, bonds, or mutual funds.

Stocks: Stocks represent ownership in a company. When you buy a stock, you become a shareholder of the company and have a claim to a portion of its assets and earnings.

Bonds: Bonds are loans that investors make to companies or governments. When you buy a bond, you are lending money to the bond issuer, and they pay you interest on the loan.

Mutual Funds: A mutual fund is a collection of stocks, bonds, or other investments that are managed by a professional fund manager. When you invest in a mutual fund, you are buying a small piece of all the investments in the fund.

Risk: Risk is the chance that you might lose money when you invest. Generally, investments that offer higher potential returns also have higher levels of risk.

Diversification: Diversification means spreading your money across different types of investments to reduce risk. By investing in a mix of stocks, bonds, and other assets, you can reduce the impact of any single investment performing poorly.

Return: Return is the amount of money you earn on your investment. Different investments offer different levels of return, and higher returns usually come with higher risk.

Asset Allocation: Asset allocation means deciding how much of your money to invest in different types of assets, such as stocks, bonds, and cash. Your asset allocation should reflect your investment goals, risk tolerance, and time horizon.

Index Funds: An index fund is a type of mutual fund that tracks a specific stock market index, such as the S&P 500. Index funds offer low costs and diversification, making them a popular choice for many investors.

Compound Interest: Compound interest is interest earned on the original investment as well as on any interest earned in previous periods. Over time, compound interest can help your investments grow significantly.

CHAPTER ONE

Setting the Foundation

Teaching kids about money management and saving

Teaching kids about money management and saving is an important life skill that will help them become financially responsible adults. Here are some tips to help parents and guardians teach their children about money:

Start early: It's never too early to start teaching your child about money. As soon as your child can count, you can start introducing them to the concept of money.

Use a clear jar to save: When teaching kids about saving, it's important to make it tangible. Use a clear jar to collect change and small bills, so kids can see their savings grow.

Make saving a game: Kids love games, so make saving money a fun activity. Set a savings goal and reward them when they reach it.

Teach them to budget: Show your child how to create a budget by dividing their money into categories such as saving, spending, and giving.

Encourage them to earn money: Help your child find ways to earn money, such as doing chores or starting a small business. This will teach them the value of hard work and the importance of earning money.

Teach them to differentiate between needs and wants: Teach your child the difference between things they need and things they want. This will help them make better spending decisions.

Discuss money openly: Talking openly about money can help kids understand how it works and how to use it wisely. Be honest about your own financial situation and talk about the importance of saving and spending wisely.

Set a good example: Children learn by example, so it's important to set a good example by being financially responsible yourself.

Teaching kids about money management and saving is a process that requires patience, consistency, and creativity. By starting early and making it fun, you can help your child develop good financial habits that will last a lifetime.

The power of compound interest

Compound interest is a powerful tool for building wealth over time, and it can be especially beneficial when investing for kids. When you invest money for a child, you are giving them the opportunity to grow their wealth over a long period of time, potentially leading to significant gains.

Compound interest occurs when the interest earned on an investment is reinvested back into the investment, allowing the investor to earn interest on their original investment as well as on the interest that has been earned. Over time, this compounding effect can lead to significant gains, especially when investing for the long term.

When investing for kids, you have a number of options. One popular choice is a tax-advantaged account such as a 529 plan, which is designed specifically for education savings. These plans allow you to invest money and grow it tax-free, as long as the money is eventually used for educational expenses.

Another option is to invest in individual stocks, mutual funds, or exchange-traded funds (ETFs). While these investments may come with more risk than a tax-advantaged account, they also offer the potential for greater returns. By choosing high-quality companies or funds and holding onto them for the long term, you can take advantage of the power of compound interest to build wealth over time.

One important thing to keep in mind when investing for kids is to start early. The longer the money is invested, the more time it has to grow and compound. Additionally, it's important to be consistent in your investing, adding money regularly to take advantage of the compounding effect.

The power of compound interest can be a valuable tool when investing for kids. By starting early, investing consistently, and choosing the right investments, you can give your child the opportunity to build significant wealth over time.

Building a financial plan

Investing for kids is a great way to set them up for a financially secure future. Here are some steps to building a financial plan for investing for kids:

Determine the investment goals: The first step is to determine the investment goals for your child. Are you investing for college tuition, a future down payment on a home, or simply for long-term financial security? The investment goals will determine the type of investments you choose.

Decide on the investment vehicles: Once you have established the investment goals, you will need to decide on the investment vehicles. You can choose between stocks, mutual funds, exchange-traded funds (ETFs), or bonds. A mix of these vehicles may be appropriate depending on your investment goals.

Establish a budget: It is important to establish a budget for your child's investment portfolio. Consider how much money you can afford to invest each month, and make sure that it fits into your overall financial plan.

Consider a tax-advantaged account: If you are investing for your child's education, consider opening a tax-advantaged account such as a 529 plan. These accounts offer tax benefits that can help you maximise your investment returns.

Monitor the investments: It is important to monitor the investments regularly to ensure that they are performing well and aligning with your investment goals. Adjustments may need to be made as your child grows and their investment needs change.

Educate your child about investing: As your child grows, it is important to educate them about investing and financial planning. Teach them the importance of saving and investing early, and help them establish good financial habits that will serve them well in the future.

Investing for kids can be a great way to help them build a secure financial future. By establishing a financial plan, choosing the right investment vehicles, and monitoring the investments regularly, you can set your child on the path to long-term financial success.

CHAPTER TWO

Investment Vehicles for Kids

Stocks

Investing in stocks can be a great way to teach kids about financial responsibility and long-term planning. Here are some things to consider when investing in stocks for kids:

Start with a small amount: Investing in stocks involves risk, and it's important to start with a small amount that you can afford to lose.

Consider index funds: Index funds are a type of mutual fund that tracks the performance of a specific index, such as the S&P 500. They are a good option for kids because they offer diversification and are less risky than individual stocks.

Invest for the long-term: Investing in stocks is a long-term game, and it's important to teach kids the value of patience and discipline. Encourage them to hold onto their investments for years or even decades.

Choose companies they know: Kids may be more interested in investing if they are familiar with the companies they are investing in. Encourage them to research and invest in companies they know and like.

Teach them about the stock market: It's important for kids to understand how the stock market works and how to read stock charts and financial statements. There are many books and online resources available to help teach kids about investing.

Consider a custodial account: A custodial account allows parents to invest on behalf of their children until they reach a certain age. This can be a good option for parents who want to manage their children's investments and teach them about the stock market.

Bonds

Investing in bonds can be a good way to teach kids about the basics of investing, and to help them develop good financial habits from a young age. Here are some key things to consider when investing in bonds for kids:

Start with education: Before you start investing, take the time to educate your child about the basics of bonds and investing. You can explain what bonds are, how they work, and why they can be a good investment option.

Choose age-appropriate investments: Depending on your child's age and risk tolerance, you can choose age-appropriate investments. For example, if your child is young, you might consider investing in U.S. savings bonds, which are very low-risk but also have low returns.

Consider a bond fund: Investing in a bond fund can be a good way to diversify your child's portfolio and potentially earn higher returns than with individual bonds. Bond funds can also provide exposure to different types of bonds, such as corporate bonds and municipal bonds.

Set realistic expectations: It's important to set realistic expectations for your child about what they can expect to earn from their investments. Make sure they understand that investing is a long-term game, and that there will be ups and downs along the way.

Use it as a learning opportunity: Investing in bonds can be a great opportunity to teach your child about money management, budgeting, and the importance of saving for the future. Make sure they are involved in the decision-making process and that they understand the risks and rewards of investing.

Remember that investing always carries some degree of risk, and there are no guarantees when it comes to returns. It's important to do your research and consult with a financial advisor before making any investment decisions.

Mutual Funds

Investing in mutual funds for kids can be a smart way to help them build long-term wealth. Mutual funds offer several benefits for young investors, including:

Diversification: Mutual funds typically invest in a range of stocks or bonds, which can help spread risk across many different companies or industries.

Professional management: Mutual funds are managed by professional fund managers who have years of experience and expertise in selecting investments.

Low minimum investment: Many mutual funds have low minimum investment requirements, which makes it easier for kids to start investing with just a small amount of money.

Automatic reinvestment: Mutual funds often automatically reinvest dividends and capital gains, which can help boost returns over time.

When investing in mutual funds for kids, it's important to choose funds that are appropriate for their age, investment goals, and risk tolerance. For younger kids, a more conservative mix of stocks and bonds may be appropriate, while older kids who have a longer investment horizon may be able to take on more risk.

It's also important to consider the fees and expenses associated with mutual funds, as these can eat into investment returns over time. Look for funds with low fees and expenses, such as index funds or exchange-traded funds (ETFs), which can provide low-cost exposure to a wide range of stocks or bonds.

Finally, it's important to educate kids about the basics of investing, including the importance of diversification, the risks and rewards of different types of investments, and the power of compound interest. By starting early and investing regularly in mutual funds, kids can build a strong foundation for long-term wealth building.

Exchange-Traded Funds (ETFs)

Exchange-Traded Funds (ETFs) can be a great option for investing for kids because they offer several benefits, such as diversification, low fees, and ease of trading. Here are some key points to keep in mind when considering ETFs for kids:

Diversification: ETFs allow investors to purchase a basket of securities, such as stocks or bonds, with just one transaction. This means that even if one of the securities in the ETF performs poorly, the overall impact on the investment will be limited. For kids who are just starting to invest, diversification can help manage risk and provide a better chance of achieving long-term growth.

Low Fees: ETFs are known for having lower fees than mutual funds or other investment vehicles. This is because they are usually passively managed, which means they track an index rather than actively trying to beat the market. This can be a great benefit for kids, who may not have as much money to invest and can benefit from minimizing fees.

Ease of Trading: ETFs are traded on stock exchanges like individual stocks, which means they can be bought and sold throughout the trading day. This makes them a convenient option for investors who want to be able to quickly adjust their portfolio as needed.

Education Opportunities: ETFs can also be a great tool for teaching kids about investing. Because they track specific sectors, industries, or indices, they can help kids understand how different parts of the market work and how different investments can perform over time. Additionally, ETFs can be a good way to start conversations about diversification and risk management.

Overall, ETFs can be a great option for investing for kids. However, as with any investment, it's important to do your research and choose ETFs that align with your child's investment goals and risk tolerance. It's also important to remember that investing comes with risk and that past performance is not a guarantee of future results.

Real Estate

Investing in real estate can be a great way to build wealth over the long-term, but it may not be the most suitable option for kids to invest in. Here are a few reasons why:

Legal Restrictions: Depending on the laws in your jurisdiction, minors may not be able to own real estate in their own name, meaning they would need an adult to act as a trustee or custodian on their behalf.

High Costs: Real estate investments typically require a large amount of capital to get started, which may not be feasible for children who don't have a significant amount of savings or earnings.

Lack of Liquidity: Real estate investments can be illiquid, meaning they can't be easily converted to cash. This can be a problem for children who may need access to their funds in the near future for education, travel or other expenses.

Maintenance and Management: Real estate investments require ongoing maintenance and management, which can be time-consuming and costly. Children may not have the skills or resources to manage these responsibilities effectively.

Instead, kids may benefit more from starting with more accessible and low-cost investments, such as savings accounts, bonds, stocks, and mutual funds. These investments are generally more liquid, require less maintenance and management, and can offer good returns over time. As children get older and gain more experience and resources, they can explore more complex investment opportunities, including real estate.

CHAPTER THREE

Risks and Rewards

Understanding the risks of investing

Investing comes with risks, and it's important to understand these risks before making any investment decisions. Here are some of the risks associated with investing:

Market Risk: Market risk refers to the risk of a decline in the value of your investments due to changes in the overall market conditions. This risk cannot be eliminated completely, but can be mitigated through diversification.

Credit Risk: Credit risk refers to the risk of default by the issuer of the security in which you have invested. This is particularly important when investing in bonds or other debt securities.

Inflation Risk: Inflation risk refers to the risk that the purchasing power of your investment may decrease over time due to inflation. This risk can be mitigated through investing in assets that have historically outpaced inflation.

Liquidity Risk: Liquidity risk refers to the risk of not being able to sell your investment when you want to or at a price that you find acceptable. This is particularly important when investing in assets that are not easily traded.

Political and Regulatory Risk: Political and regulatory risks refer to the risks associated with changes in government policies or regulations that may affect your investments.

Currency Risk: Currency risk refers to the risk of fluctuations in currency exchange rates. This risk is particularly relevant for investors who hold investments in foreign currencies.

Interest Rate Risk: Interest rate risk refers to the risk of changes in interest rates that may affect the value of your investments. This is particularly important when investing in fixed-income securities such as bonds.

It's important to carefully consider these risks before making any investment decisions. Diversification across asset classes, geographic regions, and industries can help mitigate some of these risks. Additionally, working with a financial advisor or investment professional can help you navigate these risks and make informed investment decisions.

How to manage and minimize risk

Investing for kids can be a great way to set them up for long-term financial success, but it's important to manage and minimize risk to ensure that their investments are secure. Here are some tips on how to do that:

Start with a plan: Before investing any money, it's important to have a clear plan in place. Consider your goals for the investment, the time horizon for the investment, and the level of risk you are comfortable with. This will help you choose the right investments and stay focused on your objectives.

Choose diversified investments: Diversification is key to minimizing risk in investing. Rather than putting all your money into one stock or sector, spread your investments across different asset classes, such as stocks, bonds, and real estate. This will help protect against any one investment underperforming.

Consider index funds: Index funds are a good option for kids' investments because they provide exposure to a wide range of stocks or bonds at a low cost. These funds track a specific index, such as the S&P 500, and are less risky than individual stocks.

Set up a custodial account: A custodial account allows a parent or guardian to manage investments on behalf of a child. This can be a good way to monitor the investments and ensure they are aligned with the child's goals.

Stay disciplined: It's important to stay disciplined and not let emotions drive investment decisions. Avoid making impulsive decisions based on short-term market fluctuations, and instead stick to your long-term plan.

Educate the child: Finally, it's important to educate the child about investing and help them understand the risks and rewards. This will help them make informed decisions in the future and set them up for long-term financial success.

Assessing potential rewards

Investing for kids can be a smart financial move, as it can provide them with a strong financial foundation for their future. Here are some potential rewards of investing for kids:

Compound interest: Investing at a young age can provide ample time for the investment to grow through compound interest. Compound interest means that the interest earned on the investment is reinvested, and as a result, the investment grows faster over time.

Long-term growth: Investing in stocks or other long-term assets can provide substantial growth over the long-term. While there may be short-term fluctuations in the market, investing in quality assets with a long-term outlook can result in significant returns.

Financial education: Investing for kids can also provide an opportunity for them to learn about money management and investing early on. By involving them in the investment process, they can learn about the benefits of investing, and how to make informed investment decisions.

Tax benefits: Investing for kids can also provide tax benefits, such as the ability to take advantage of tax-advantaged accounts like 529 plans or UTMA/UGMA accounts.

Investing for kids can provide significant rewards in the long-term, including compound interest, long-term growth, financial education, and tax benefits. However, it's important to note that investing involves risk, and it's important to consult with a financial advisor to determine the best investment strategy for your child's specific needs and goals.

CHAPTER FOUR

Teaching Kids to Invest

Strategies for teaching kids about investing

Teaching kids about investing is a great way to help them develop financial literacy and become financially responsible adults. Here are some strategies for teaching kids about investing:

Start with the basics: Teach kids about the different types of investments, such as stocks, bonds, mutual funds, and real estate. Explain how each type works and the risks and rewards associated with them.

Use real-life examples: Use real-life examples of companies they know, such as Apple, Disney, or Nike, to explain how investing works. Show them how the stock prices fluctuate and how their investment can grow over time.

Start small: Encourage kids to start small by investing in low-risk investments such as index funds. Show them how to research investments and how to diversify their portfolio.

Make it fun: Make investing fun by using games or simulations that teach kids about investing. You can also give them a small amount of money to invest and track their progress.

Teach the value of patience: Teach kids the value of patience when it comes to investing. Explain that investments take time to grow and that they should avoid making impulsive decisions based on short-term fluctuations in the market.

Encourage questions: Encourage kids to ask questions about investing and provide them with resources, such as books or online tutorials, to help them learn more.

Lead by example: Finally, lead by example by showing your kids how you invest and manage your own finances. This will help them understand the importance of financial responsibility and inspire them to make smart financial decisions in the future.

Age-appropriate approaches

Investing can be a valuable tool for kids to learn about money management, saving, and financial responsibility. However, it's important to approach investing in an age-appropriate way to ensure that kids understand the basics and can make informed decisions. Here are some age-appropriate approaches to investing for kids:

Ages 5-8: Introduce the concept of saving money and explain how it can grow over time. Encourage kids to save their allowance or birthday money in a piggy bank or savings account. Talk about the benefits of delayed gratification and how small amounts can add up over time.

Ages 9-12: Teach kids about the different types of investments, such as stocks, bonds, and mutual funds. Explain how they work and the risks and rewards associated with each. Encourage them to research companies or funds they are interested in and track their performance.

Ages 13-15: Help kids open a custodial brokerage account and start investing in stocks or mutual funds with a small amount of money. Teach them how to read stock charts and financial statements and encourage them to diversify their investments.

Ages 16-18: Introduce more advanced investing concepts such as options trading, short selling, and margin trading. Teach them about the importance of a long-term investment strategy and the potential benefits of compounding returns.

Regardless of age, it's important to emphasize the importance of investing in a responsible and informed way. Encourage kids to do their research, seek advice from trusted adults, and always consider the risks before making any investment decisions.

Encouraging healthy investing habits

Developing healthy investing habits is essential to achieving long-term financial goals. Here are some tips to encourage healthy investing habits:

Start with a plan: Create a well-defined investment plan that outlines your financial goals, risk tolerance, and investment strategy.

Diversify your portfolio: Diversification is the key to minimizing risk and maximizing returns. Invest in a variety of assets classes, such as stocks, bonds, real estate, and commodities.

Invest for the long-term: Investing for the long-term provides the best opportunity to achieve your financial goals. Avoid short-term speculation and focus on long-term growth.

Stick to your plan: Don't let short-term market fluctuations or emotional decisions derail your investment plan. Stay disciplined and stick to your investment plan.

Continuously educate yourself: Keep learning about investing and finance. Read books, attend seminars, and consult with financial advisors to stay informed and make informed investment decisions.

Regularly monitor your investments: Regularly review your investments to ensure they are aligned with your goals and risk tolerance. Rebalance your portfolio if necessary to maintain your desired asset allocation.

Start early: The earlier you start investing, the more time your money has to grow. Start as early as possible and let the power of compound interest work for you.

CHAPTER FIVE

Encouraging Long-Term Thinking

The benefits of long-term investing

Long-term investing can be a great way to help kids build wealth and secure their financial future. Here are some of the benefits of long-term investing for kids:

Compounding returns: When you invest money, you earn returns on that investment. Over time, those returns can compound, which means you earn returns on your returns. This can lead to significant growth over the long term.

Time in the market: The longer you stay invested, the more time your money has to grow. By starting early and investing regularly, kids can take advantage of the power of compounding returns and time in the market.

Reduced risk: Investing in the stock market can be risky in the short term, but over the long term, the market tends to trend upwards. By investing for the long term, kids can reduce the risk of short-term market volatility.

Education: Investing can be a great way to teach kids about financial literacy, economics, and how to make informed decisions about money.

Goal-setting: Investing can help kids set financial goals and work towards them over time. This can teach them valuable skills like budgeting, saving, and planning for the future.

Long-term investing can be a powerful tool for helping kids build wealth, learn about money, and secure their financial future.

Teaching kids to think about the future

Teaching kids to think about the future is an important aspect of their education and personal development. Here are some ways to encourage children to think about the future:

Help them understand the concept of time: Start by explaining to children the concept of time, and how it can be divided into the past, present, and future. Use examples that are relevant to their lives, such as how they have grown and changed over time, and what they can do to plan for the future.

Encourage them to set goals: Encourage children to set both short-term and long-term goals for themselves. This could include goals related to school, sports, hobbies, or personal growth. Help them develop a plan to achieve these goals, and celebrate their successes along the way.

Talk about the consequences of actions: Help children understand that the choices they make today can have an impact on their future. For example, if they neglect their homework or skip classes, it can affect their grades and future opportunities. Similarly, if they make healthy choices today, they are more likely to stay healthy and active in the future.

Discuss future possibilities: Talk to children about the different possibilities that exist in their future, and help them explore their interests and passions. Encourage them to think about what they might want to do when they grow up, and what steps they can take to pursue their dreams.

Teach them to plan ahead: Help children develop the habit of planning ahead by showing them how to use a calendar or planner to keep track of important dates and events. Encourage them to think about what they need to do to prepare for upcoming tests or projects, and how they can manage their time effectively.

By encouraging children to think about the future, you are helping them develop important life skills that will serve them well in the years to come.

Patience and discipline

Teaching kids about patience and discipline in investing is a valuable lesson that can set them up for financial success later in life. Here are some tips to help you instill these important qualities in your child:

Start early: The earlier your child starts investing, the more time they have to grow their wealth.

Encourage them to start saving and investing as soon as they can.

Set goals: Help your child set realistic goals for their investments. This will help them stay focused and motivated, and give them a sense of purpose.

Be consistent: Encourage your child to invest regularly, even if it's just a small amount each month. Consistency is key when it comes to building wealth over time.

Teach them about risk: Investing always involves some level of risk, and it's important for your child to understand this. Teach them about diversification and the importance of spreading their investments across different asset classes.

Celebrate successes: When your child achieves their investment goals, celebrate their successes with them. This will reinforce the value of patience and discipline in investing, and help them stay motivated to continue investing in the future.

By teaching your child about patience and discipline in investing, you can help them build a solid financial foundation for the rest of their life.

CHAPTER SIX

Supporting Your Kids' Investing Journey

Encouraging and supporting your kids' interest in investing

Investing can be a valuable skill for kids to learn, as it can help them develop financial literacy and long-term financial planning skills.

Here are some tips for encouraging and supporting your kids' interest in investing:

Start with the basics: Before your kids start investing, make sure they have a basic understanding of financial concepts like saving, budgeting, and compound interest. This will help them make informed investment decisions.

Lead by example: Set a good example by talking openly about your own investments and financial decisions. This will help your kids see the value of investing and encourage them to ask questions.

Make it fun: Investing can seem like a daunting topic to kids, so try to make it fun and engaging. Play games like Monopoly or Stock Market Game to help them learn about investing in a more interactive and exciting way.

Open a custodial account: Consider opening a custodial account for your kids that will allow them to invest in stocks, bonds, and other securities. This will give them hands-on experience with investing and allow them to see how their investments perform over time.

Use real-life examples: Help your kids understand how investing works in the real world by using real-life examples. For instance, you could explain how Warren Buffet invests or how a company's stock price changes over time.

Teach risk management: It's important for kids to learn about risk management when it comes to investing. Help them understand the risks associated with different types of investments and how to diversify their portfolio to minimise risk.

Emphasise long-term investing: Encourage your kids to think long-term when it comes to investing. Explain how investing early can help them grow their wealth over time and how patience is key when it comes to investing.

Resources and tools for kids to learn about investing

Here are some resources and tools that kids can use to learn about investing:

Stock market games: Websites like Virtual Stock Exchange, Wall Street Survivor, and Investopedia have stock market games that allow kids to simulate investing in the stock market with fake money.

Books: There are many books available that explain investing in simple terms for kids. Some examples include "Growing Money: A Complete Investing Guide for Kids" by Gail Karlitz and Debbie Honig, and "The Young Investor: Projects and Activities for Making Your Money Grow" by Katherine R. Bateman.

Online courses: Websites like Udemy, Coursera, and Khan Academy offer online courses on investing that are suitable for kids.

Robo-advisors: Platforms like Acorns Early, Stockpile, and Stash have robo-advisors that allow kids to invest in stocks and ETFs with as little as $5.

Financial literacy programs: Organizations like Junior Achievement, The National Endowment for Financial Education, and The Mint offer financial literacy programs and resources for kids.

Parental guidance: The best resource for kids to learn about investing is often their parents. Parents can teach kids about saving, budgeting, and investing, and help them understand the different investment options available.

Partnering with financial professionals

Investing for kids can be a great way to help them build long-term wealth and financial security. Partnering with financial professionals can be helpful in making informed investment decisions.

Here are some things to keep in mind when investing for kids with the help of financial professionals:

Choose the right financial professional: Look for a financial professional who has experience working with families and investing for children. Consider their credentials, experience, and reputation in the industry.

Determine your goals: Be clear about your goals for the investment. Do you want to save for college, help your child start a business, or provide for their future financial security? This will help the financial professional recommend the right investment vehicles for your needs.

Consider the child's age: The investment strategy will differ depending on the child's age. For younger children, long-term investments may be more appropriate, while for older children, you may want to focus on shorter-term investments to help them build savings for immediate needs.

Discuss risk tolerance: It's important to discuss your risk tolerance with the financial professional, as this will determine the investment strategy. If you're risk-averse, you may want to focus on more conservative investments, while if you're comfortable with risk, you may want to explore higher-risk investment options.

Choose the right investment vehicles: There are a variety of investment vehicles available, including stocks, mutual funds, exchange-traded funds (ETFs), and bonds. Your financial professional can help you determine the best options based on your goals and risk tolerance.

Monitor the investment: It's important to monitor the investment regularly and make adjustments as needed. This can include rebalancing the portfolio or adjusting the investment strategy as the child grows older.

Overall, partnering with financial professionals can help you make informed decisions when investing for kids. By working with a professional, you can develop a strategy that aligns with your goals and helps you provide for your child's financial future.

CONCLUSION

Investing is an excellent way for kids to learn about financial management and grow their money over time. By investing early in life, they can take advantage of compound interest, which means their money can grow even faster. It also helps them develop a long-term financial mindset and the discipline to stick to their financial goals.

Here are some tips and encouragement for kids to start investing:

Start small: Kids don't need a lot of money to start investing. They can begin with just a few dollars, and as they learn more about investing, they can increase their investments.

Do your research: Encourage kids to learn about different types of investments and understand the risks involved. There are many resources available online, including books and articles, that can help kids learn more about investing.

Set financial goals: Setting financial goals can help kids stay motivated and focused. Encourage them to set both short-term and long-term goals, and to track their progress over time.

Be patient: Investing is a long-term strategy, and it takes time to see significant growth. Encourage kids to be patient and not get discouraged if they don't see immediate results.

Seek guidance: Encourage kids to seek guidance from parents, teachers, or other trusted adults. They can also consider working with a financial advisor to help them develop a personalised investment strategy.

Investing can be a rewarding and educational experience for kids. By starting early and taking a long-term approach, they can set themselves up for financial success in the future.

www.ingramcontent.com/pod-product-compliance
Lightning Source LLC
Chambersburg PA
CBHW071048220526
45467CB00004B/1734